First published in
Great Britain in 1984 by
Franklin Watts
12a Golden Square
London W1

First published in the
United States in 1984 by
Gloucester Press

Copyright © Aladdin Books Ltd 1984

Printed in Belgium

ISBN 0–531–03482–8

Library of Congress Catalog
Card Number: 84–81109

WRITE YOUR OWN PROGRAM

BEGINNING BASIC

SPACE JOURNEY

Gary Marshall

GLOUCESTER PRESS

NEW YORK · TORONTO · 1984

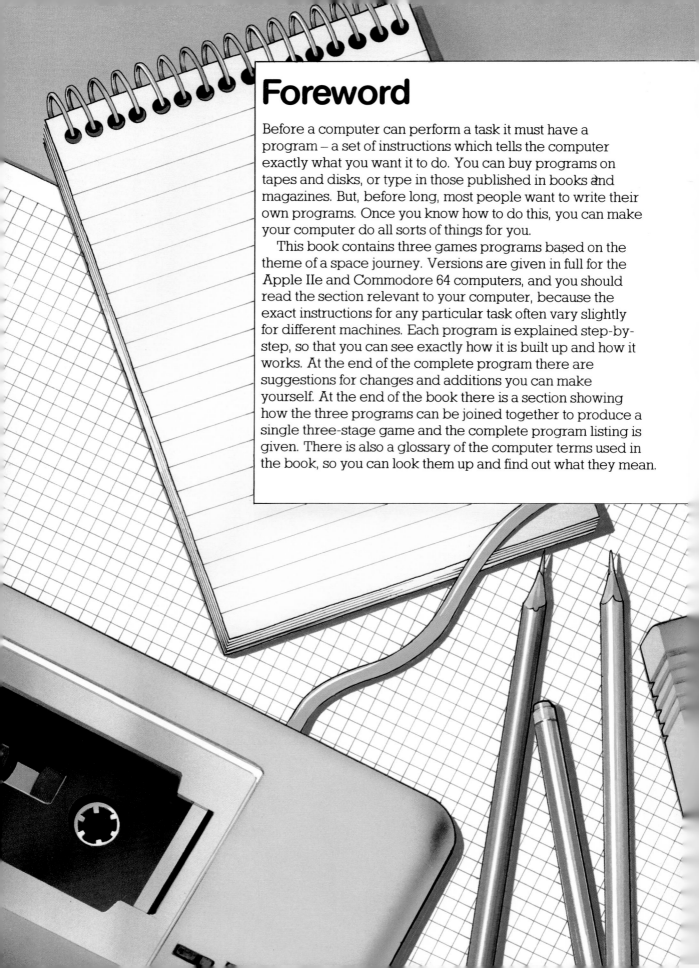

Foreword

Before a computer can perform a task it must have a program – a set of instructions which tells the computer exactly what you want it to do. You can buy programs on tapes and disks, or type in those published in books and magazines. But, before long, most people want to write their own programs. Once you know how to do this, you can make your computer do all sorts of things for you.

This book contains three games programs based on the theme of a space journey. Versions are given in full for the Apple IIe and Commodore 64 computers, and you should read the section relevant to your computer, because the exact instructions for any particular task often vary slightly for different machines. Each program is explained step-by-step, so that you can see exactly how it is built up and how it works. At the end of the complete program there are suggestions for changes and additions you can make yourself. At the end of the book there is a section showing how the three programs can be joined together to produce a single three-stage game and the complete program listing is given. There is also a glossary of the computer terms used in the book, so you can look them up and find out what they mean.

Contents

```
20 D=18000:S=400:H=2000:F=5
30 C$="              "
40 PRINT TAB(2,1)CHR$129"HEIGHT   "CHR$132"DESCENT   "
   CHR$131"SPEED   "CHR$133"DISTANCE"
50 PRINT TAB(35,23)CHR$146CHR$255CHR$255CHR$255
60 X=0:Y=4
70 PRINT TAB(X,Y)CHR$146CHR$255CHR$255CHR$255
80 PRINT TAB(3,2)CHR$150CHR$253CHR$252CHR$244
90 PRINT TAB(3,2)C$
100 PRINT TAB(3,2)CHR$129;H
110 PRINT TAB(13,2)C$
120 PRINT TAB(13,2)CHR$132;F
130 PRINT TAB(22,2)C$
140 PRINT TAB(22,2)CHR$131;S
150 PRINT TAB(30,2)C$
160 IF S<200 T...CHR...
```

Introducing BASIC

Most programs for home computers are written in a computer language called BASIC. Just like any other language, BASIC has rules that have to be followed if the program is to work. For example, the BASIC command **PRINT** causes information to be displayed on the screen. But text to be displayed must be enclosed between double quotation marks, as in the first line of program shown below. Try the other lines and see what happens. You'll notice lines two and three produce very different results because the computer treats figures differently from words. The BASIC arithmetic symbols are shown on the notepad below.

```
PRINT "HAPPY BIRTHDAY"
PRINT "15*2"
PRINT  15*2
```

With a complete program, the computer must perform each instruction in a logical order. Also, a program wouldn't work if the computer performed each instruction as soon as it was typed in. By giving each instruction a line number, we tell the computer to store it in its memory until the program is **RUN**. Line numbers usually go up in steps of ten, so that the first three lines of program are often numbered 10, 20, and 30. The computer carries out each instruction in strict numerical order, and additional instructions can be added afterwards by giving them line numbers such as 15, 25 and so on, as appropriate. Try typing in the short program below. Notice that line 10 does not appear on the screen. The **REM** command is short for reminder, and the computer ignores anything placed after it.

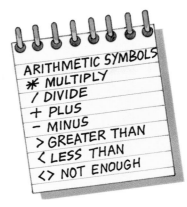

ARITHMETIC SYMBOLS
* MULTIPLY
/ DIVIDE
+ PLUS
− MINUS
> GREATER THAN
< LESS THAN
<> NOT ENOUGH

```
10 REM "BIRTHDAY GREETING"
20 PRINT "HAPPY BIRTHDAY TO YOU"
30 PRINT "HAPPY BIRTHDAY TO YOU"
40 PRINT "HAPPY BIRTHDAY DEAR COMPUTER"
50 PRINT "HAPPY BIRTHDAY TO YOU"
60 PRINT
70 PRINT "YOU ARE"
80 PRINT "1"
90 PRINT "YEAR OLD"
```

```
HAPPY BIRTHDAY TO YOU
HAPPY BIRTHDAY TO YOU
HAPPY BIRTHDAY DEAR COMPUTER
HAPPY BIRTHDAY TO YOU

YOU ARE
1
YEAR OLD
```

RUN RETURN

Getting to know your computer

Before you begin to work on any of the programs, it is a good idea to experiment with your computer so that you get to know the keyboard. It doesn't matter what you type in – you can't do the computer any harm. Most often the computer will respond with "? Syntax error" or "Illegal quantity." These messages – called error messages – are very useful when you know more about programming, but for beginners it's best to ignore them.

   In particular, learn how to use the editing keys so that you can erase any mistakes you might make. The manuals that are supplied with the computer will help you to use these. Don't worry if there are certain keys you don't understand – you'll get to know what they do when you need them. Below some of the most important keys and instructions are highlighted.

N.B. The keys colored red below are applicable to both the Apple IIe and Commodore. Blue Keys apply to the Commodore only.

This key (short for **CONTROL**) has a number of functions on both computers. On the Commodore it is used to obtain the first eight colors available, and on the Apple, **CNTRL** used with the **"C"** key stops a program running. See the user's manuals for more detail on **CONTROL** functions.

This is the Commodore logo key and has a number of functions. It gives access to the second eight colors available and to the graphics symbols on the bottom left of each key.

This key on the Commodore stops a program while it is running. If the program is waiting for an **INPUT**, then you must press this key and then the **RESTORE** key to stop a program.

On the Apple, the **DEL**ete key is used in conjunction with the cursor keys to correct errors. On the Commodore, **INST DEL** deletes the character to the left of the cursor. Used with the **SHIFT** key, **INST DEL** inserts spaces into a program line.

This selects either lower case or capital letters. Capitals are obtained when the **SHIFT LOCK** is down. All programming commands and instructions should be typed in in capital letters.

This key must be used to enter program lines into the computer's memory after they have been typed in. It is also used to make the computer execute commands such as **RUN**, **LIST** and **SAVE**.

This key positions the cursor at the top left-hand corner of the screen. Used with the **SHIFT** key, **CLR/HOME** clears the screen and places the cursor in this home position.

Preparing a program

Before you begin writing a program in BASIC, you should know exactly what it is you want the computer to do. The first stage is to write an outline for your program in ordinary English. For example, the outline for the first program in this book might read: "Idea of game is to guess a random number. If guess is correct then computer shows a shuttle lift off display. No more than 10 guesses. Instructions for playing should be clearly displayed on the screen."

You should also plan how you want the screen to look so that any instructions are clearly displayed. Graph paper is useful for this, because the computer's screen is also divided into vertical and horizontal coordinates, although the exact number of these varies from machine to machine. The initial planning for the second game in this book, in which you have to pilot the shuttle through a field of asteroids, is shown on the notepad opposite and a basic screen plan is also given. Once these preparations are made you can go on to the next stage – drawing up a flowchart. The flowchart will enable you to break down your plan into each of the logical steps contained within the program you wish to write.

ASTEROIDS IN RANDOM POSITIONS. SHUTTLE STARTS ON THE LEFT. SHUTTLE CAN MOVE UP, DOWN AND RIGHT ACROSS THE SCREEN. GAME ENDS IF SHUTTLE CRASHES INTO AN ASTEROID OR GOES OFF SCREEN. MESSAGES TO APPEAR FOR SUCCESS OR FAILURE.

INSTRUCTIONS

SHUTTLE START POSITION

ASTEROID BELT

SHUTTLE'S OBJECTIVE

Flowchart

Flowcharts break problems down into sets of decisions and instructions. The flowchart shown below is for the first program in the book. The diamond-shaped boxes indicate points at which decisions are taken – is the guess too high, for example, or have you used up ten guesses? The questions are always answered yes or no and depending on the answer the next appropriate step is taken. Square boxes are used to indicate points at which operations are made, such as for the initial screen display. Flowcharts help you to ask the right questions, so that you can give the correct instructions to the computer. By carefully studying the flowchart it's possible to see if any stages have been left out. Once the flowchart works, all that remains to do is to convert each section into the programming commands of the BASIC language.

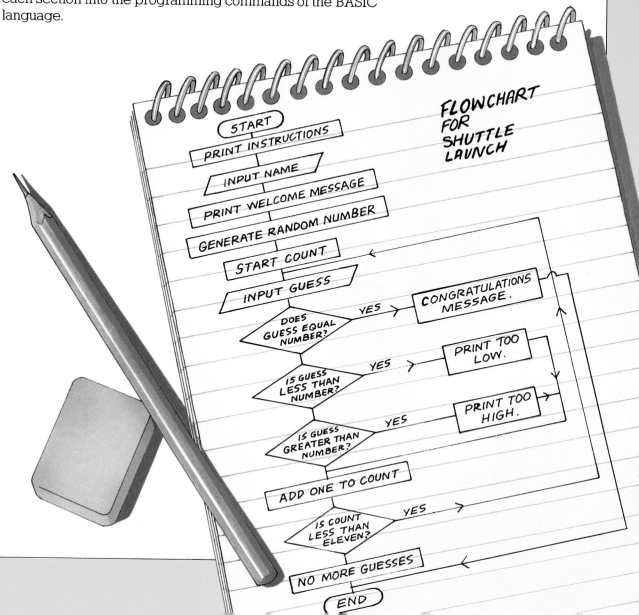

FLOWCHART FOR SHUTTLE LAUNCH

START

PRINT INSTRUCTIONS

INPUT NAME

PRINT WELCOME MESSAGE

GENERATE RANDOM NUMBER

START COUNT

INPUT GUESS

DOES GUESS EQUAL NUMBER? — YES → CONGRATULATIONS MESSAGE.

IS GUESS LESS THAN NUMBER? — YES → PRINT TOO LOW.

IS GUESS GREATER THAN NUMBER? — YES → PRINT TOO HIGH.

ADD ONE TO COUNT

IS COUNT LESS THAN ELEVEN? — YES →

NO MORE GUESSES

END

Saving programs on tape

No matter how well you get to know a program, it is very time-consuming to type it into your computer, line-by-line each time you want to **RUN** it. And, quite probably, you'll make typing errors, so that the program will need careful checking and correcting, or "debugging," as it is called in computer jargon. So once you have the program working, you'll want to be able to store it on tape for future use. This is a simple procedure and the instructions for saving and loading programs are given on the notepads below. It's a good idea to save two versions of your program before switching your computer off, just in case the first one hasn't recorded properly, which sometimes happens. Make the first recording and then wind the tape on for, say, ten turns before the second recording. Label your tape with the program name and its position: "Takeoff 10" for the first version and "Takeoff 20" for the second and so on. For this reason, it's important to remember to set the counter on the tape recorder to zero before you begin. With properly labeled tapes, you can go straight to your program when you want to use it again.

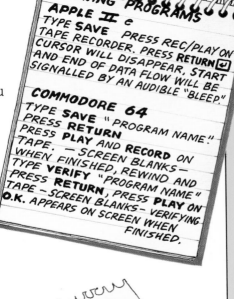

SAVING PROGRAMS

APPLE II e
TYPE **SAVE**   PRESS REC/PLAY ON TAPE RECORDER. PRESS **RETURN** ↵ CURSOR WILL DISAPPEAR, START AND END OF DATA FLOW WILL BE SIGNALLED BY AN AUDIBLE "BLEEP."

COMMODORE 64
TYPE **SAVE** " PROGRAM NAME".
PRESS **RETURN**
PRESS **PLAY** AND **RECORD** ON TAPE. — SCREEN BLANKS—
WHEN FINISHED, REWIND AND TYPE **VERIFY** " PROGRAM NAME "
PRESS **RETURN**, PRESS **PLAY** ON TAPE. – SCREEN BLANKS – VERIFYING.
O.K. APPEARS ON SCREEN WHEN FINISHED.

LOADING PROGRAMS
APPLE II e
TYPE **LOAD**   PRESS **PLAY** ON TAPE RECORDER. PRESS **RETURN** CURSOR WILL DISAPPEAR. START AND END OF DATA FLOW WILL BE SIGNALLED BY AN AUDIBLE "BLEEP"

COMMODORE 64
TYPE **"LOAD"** PRESS **RETURN**. PRESS **PLAY** ON TAPE – SCREEN BLANKS– SCREEN REAPPEARS–" FOUND PROGRAM NAME "MESSAGE. PRESS CBM LOGO KEY, OR WAIT 30 SECONDS– SCREEN BLANKS– SCREEN REAPPEARS – LOADED !

SHUTTLE LAUNCH

You are the commander of the space shuttle. To launch the shuttle, you must input the required power level to the shuttle's central computer. You have only ten attempts to guess the correct level or the mission is aborted. The computer will tell you if your guess is too high or too low. If you succeed, the shuttle's instrument panel will show your height increasing until orbit is achieved. Good luck!

```
WELCOME ABOARD CAPTAIN GORDON

TO LAUNCH THE SHUTTLE YOU MUST
GUESS THE POWER LEVEL REQUIRED
(ANY NUMBER BETWEEN 1 AND 100)

TYPE IT IN AND PRESS RETURN
GO AHEAD, PLEASE

50

TOO HIGH, TRY AGAIN
```

This program uses the computer's ability to generate random numbers. Most of the program lines consist of the instructions given to the player during the game. The first nine lines of program create the initial display.

```
5    REM   SHUTTLE LAUNCH
10    TEXT : HOME
20    VTAB 4: HTAB 13: PRINT "SHUTTLE LAUNCH"
30    HTAB 13: PRINT "----------------"
40    VTAB 8: HTAB 3: PRINT "THE SHUTTLE IS READY FOR
      LIFT OFF"
50    VTAB 10: HTAB 3: PRINT "YOUR TASK IS TO LAUNCH
      IT"
60    VTAB 13: HTAB 3: PRINT "YOU MAY HAVE ONLY TEN
      ATTEMPTS!!"
70    VTAB 16: HTAB 3: PRINT "PLEASE ENTER YOUR NAME"
80    VTAB 18: HTAB 3: PRINT "BY TYPING IT AND PRESSING
      RETURN"
```

Line 5 gives the program its title, using the **REM** statement, **TEXT** mode is selected and the screen is cleared using the **HOME** command in line 10. **VTAB** and **HTAB** instructions are used to position the information on the screen. **VTAB** controls the vertical position, and is followed by a number ranging from 1 for the top line of the screen, to 24 for the bottom. **HTAB** controls the horizontal position, and should be followed by 1 for the left-hand side of the screen, to 40, for the right-hand side. So in line 20, **"SHUTTLE LAUNCH"** is positioned four lines down, thirteen spaces across. The other instructions are similarly positioned.

VTAB 4 POSITIONS THE CURSOR ON THE 4th LINE DOWN. HTAB 13 POSITIONS THE CURSOR ON THE 13th POSITION ACROSS.

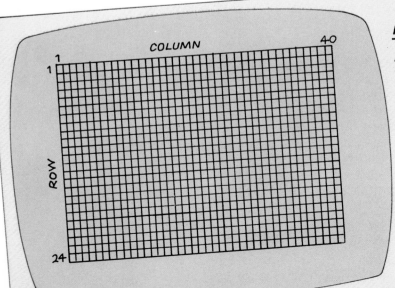

IN TEXT MODE THE SCREEN SIZE IS 24 ROWS BY 40 COLUMNS. TEXT IS POSITIONED BY VTAB AND HTAB STATEMENTS.

```
85    VTAB 20: HTAB 3
90    INPUT NA$
100   HOME
110   HTAB 4: PRINT "WELCOME ABOARD, CAPTAIN ";NA$
120   VTAB 8: HTAB 5: PRINT "TO LAUNCH THE SHUTTLE YOU
      MUST"
130   VTAB 10: HTAB 5: PRINT "GUESS THE POWER LEVEL
140   VTAB 12: HTAB 5: PRINT "(ANY NUMBER BETWEEN 1
      AND 100)"
150   VTAB 14: HTAB 5: PRINT "TYPE IT IN AND PRESS
      RETURN"
160   VTAB 16: HTAB 12: PRINT "GO AHEAD,
      PLEASE"
```

Next, line 90 enables the player's name to be entered while the program is running – line 85 places the cursor in a suitable position. The **INPUT** command causes a question mark to appear on the screen. Whatever is typed in will be placed in a *string variable* called **NA$**. The string sign, **$**, tells the computer to expect letters and/or numbers as input. The computer displays the **INPUT** when asked to **PRINT NA$**, as in line 110. Notice that **NA$** is outside the quotation marks. After the **INPUT**, the screen is cleared in line 100, and the second set of instructions is displayed.

SPACE

"TOO LOW, TRY AGAIN"
"TOO HIGH, TRY AGAIN"
THE SPACE IN LINE 210
OVERPRINTS THE EXTRA
LETTER IN THE MESSAGE
PRINTED BY LINE 220.

```
170   LET LEV =   INT ( RND (1)  *  100) + 1
180   FOR A = 1 TO 10
190   VTAB 19: HTAB 18:  INPUT GU
200   IF GU = LEV THEN   GOTO 280
205   VTAB 21: HTAB 10
210   IF GU < LEV THEN   PRINT "TOO LOW, TRY AGAIN "
220   IF GU > LEV THEN   PRINT "TOO HIGH, TRY AGAIN"
230   NEXT A
240   HOME
250   VTAB 10: HTAB 2: PRINT "YOU HAVE FAILED AFTER
      TEN ATTEMPTS!!"
260   VTAB 12: HTAB 1: PRINT "TYPE 'RUN' AND PRESS
      RETURN TO TRY AGAIN"
270   STOP
```

In line 170, **RND(1)**, produces a random number between 0 and 1. This is multiplied by 100 and made a whole number using **INT** and is stored in the variable **LEV**. Line 180 sets up **A** to count from 1 to 10, to limit the number of guesses. Line 200 checks for a correct guess and lines 210 and 220 tell the player if the guess was too low or too high. After ten attempts, the program goes to lines 240 to 260 and the game ends.

```
280    HOME
290    LET HE = 0
300    LET TA = 10000
310    VTAB 5: HTAB 13: PRINT "LIFT-OFF!!!"
320    VTAB 10: HTAB 10: PRINT "HEIGHT"
330    VTAB 10: HTAB 20: PRINT HE
340    FOR DE = 1 TO 500
350    NEXT DE
360    LET HE = HE * 2 + 1
370    IF HE < TA GOTO 330
```

The liftoff display shows the shuttle's height on the "instrument panel" increasing as the shuttle accelerates to reach orbit. Line 290 sets the takeoff height at zero and line 300 sets the target for the orbit at 10,000. The next three lines display the words LIFT OFF and HEIGHT and the figure for height at the desired positions on the screen, to form the instrument panel. Line 360 calculates the changing height by doubling the old figure and adding one. Because the computer works so fast, the changing figures for the height would flash past on the screen too quickly to be seen clearly if the computer were allowed simply to make the calculations and display them. To slow the computer down, a delay loop is added at lines 340 and 350. These commands in effect tell the computer to count to 500 before doing anything else. Line 370 instructs the computer to go back to line 330, display the figure obtained for height and run through to obtain a new value for height. This is repeated until the figure obtained for height is greater than the target set for achieving orbit.

TAKE CARE WITH PUNCTUATION. IN LINE 420, A SEMI-COLON (;) TELLS THE COMPUTER TO **PRINT NA$** DIRECTLY AFTER THE MESSAGE.

```
380    HOME
390    FOR RO = 10 TO 15
400    VTAB RO: HTAB 11: PRINT "SHUTTLE IN ORBIT!!!!"
410    NEXT RO
420    VTAB 19: HTAB 2: PRINT "CONGRATULATIONS
       CAPTAIN ";NA$
430    END
```

The final section of the program displays the congratulatory message. It uses a **FOR......NEXT** loop in lines 390 to 410 as an easy way of printing "SHUTTLE IN ORBIT" five times. It works by using **RO** as a variable used in the **VTAB** instruction, having values ranging from 10 to 15. In effect, it tells the computer to print on each screen row, from row 10 to row 15. Without this loop, it would be necessary to copy line 400 six times, with a different program line for each row.

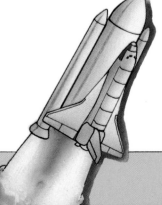

This program uses the computer's ability to generate random numbers. Most of the program lines consist of instructions to the player that will appear on the screen at appropriate moments during the game. The first nine lines of program create the initial display.

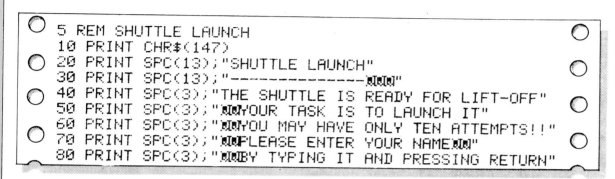

```
5 REM SHUTTLE LAUNCH
10 PRINT CHR$(147)
20 PRINT SPC(13);"SHUTTLE LAUNCH"
30 PRINT SPC(13);"---------------◖◗◖◗"
40 PRINT SPC(3);"THE SHUTTLE IS READY FOR LIFT-OFF"
50 PRINT SPC(3);"◖◗YOUR TASK IS TO LAUNCH IT"
60 PRINT SPC(3);"◖◗YOU MAY HAVE ONLY TEN ATTEMPTS!!"
70 PRINT SPC(3);"◖◗PLEASE ENTER YOUR NAME◖◗◖◗"
80 PRINT SPC(3);"◖◗BY TYPING IT AND PRESSING RETURN"
```

In line 10, the screen is cleared using **CHR$(147)**. To make all the text appear near the middle of the screen, the **SPC** command (short for space) is used. **SPC** is always followed by the number of spaces that should appear before the printing starts, given in parenthesis. To position the information down the screen, cursor control codes are used. These are available by typing first a set of double quotation marks and then pressing the "up/down" cursor key. This causes a reversed "Q" symbol to appear on the screen, instead of moving the cursor. So in line 30, the three cursor control symbols place three line spaces between the underlining and the next message printed in line 40. In lines 50 to 80 the cursor control symbols appear before the message to be printed, to give two line spaces.

"PRINT CHR $ (147)" CLEARS THE SCREEN. THE CURSOR CONTROL CODE FOR THE SAME THING IS A REVERSED HEART.

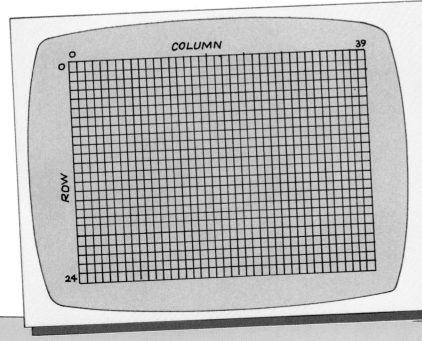

DRAW THE COMMODORE SCREEN GRID TO PLOT HOW YOU WANT THE SCREEN TO LOOK BEFORE PROGRAMMING.

```
90 INPUT NA$
100 PRINT CHR$(147)
110 PRINT "█WELCOME ABOARD,CAPTAIN ";NA$
120 PRINT SPC(5);"█TO LAUNCH THE SHUTTLE YOU MUST"
130 PRINT SPC(5)"█GUESS THE POWER LEVEL REQUIRED"
140 PRINT SPC(5)"█(ANY NUMBER BETWEEN 1 AND 100)"
150 PRINT SPC(6)"█TYPE IT IN AND PRESS RETURN"
160 PRINT SPC(12)"█GO AHEAD,PLEASE"
```

Line 90 allows the player's name to be entered while the program is running. The **INPUT** command causes a question mark and flashing cursor to appear on the screen to prompt the user. The input typed in is placed in a *string variable* labeled **NA$**. The string sign **$** tells the computer to accept both letters and numbers as input. The computer displays the **INPUT** when asked to **PRINT NA$**, as in line 110. Notice that the string sign lies outside the quotation marks and is preceded by a semi-colon. After the **INPUT**, the screen is cleared by line 100, and the second set of instructions contained in lines 110 to 160 is displayed.

SPACE

"...TOO LOW, TRY AGAIN"
"...TOO HIGH, TRY AGAIN"

THE SPACE IN LINE 210 OVERPRINTS THE EXTRA LETTER IN THE MESSAGE PRINTED BY LINE 220.

```
170 LE=INT(RND(0)*100)+1
180 FOR AT=1 TO 10
190 INPUT "     ████";GU
200 IF GU=LE THEN GOTO 280
210 IF GU<LE THEN PRINT SPC(7);GU;".. TOO LOW, TRY
    ▀AGAIN"
220 IF GU>LE THEN PRINT SPC(7);GU;"..TOO HIGH, TRY
    ▀AGAIN"
230 NEXT AT
240 PRINT CHR$(147)
250 PRINT SPC(2);"█████████YOU HAVE FAILED AFTER TEN
    ATTEMPTS!!"
260 PRINT"█TYPE 'RUN' AND PRESS RETURN TO TRY AGAIN"
270 STOP
```

The **RND(0)** command in line 170 generates a random number between 0 and 1. This is multiplied by 100 and made a whole number, or integer, using **INT**. Because **INT** rounds down to the nearest whole number, a 1 is added to make sure the figure can never be zero. This number is stored in the variable **LE** (short for level). Line 180 limits the number of guesses to ten. If the guess is correct, then the program goes to the success display at line 280, otherwise lines 210 and 220 tell the player if the guess was too low or too high. After ten attempts, the program goes through to lines 240 to 260 and the relevant messages are printed.

```
280 PRINT CHR$(147)
290 HI=0
300 TA=10000
310 PRINT SPC(14);"█████LIFT-OFF!!!!"
320 PRINT SPC(15);"████HEIGHT███"
330 PRINT SPC(16);"⌐"HI
340 FOR DE=1 TO 500
350 NEXT DE
360 HI=HI*2+1
370 IF HI<TA THEN GOTO 330
```

The liftoff display shows the shuttle's height on the "instrument panel" increasing as the shuttle accelerates to reach its orbit. Line 290 sets the takeoff height at zero and line 300 sets the target for the orbit at 10,000. The next three lines display the words LIFT OFF and HEIGHT and the figure for height at the desired positions on the screen to form the instrument panel. Line 360 calculates the changing height by doubling the old figure and adding one. Because the computer works so fast, the figures for the height would flash past on the screen too quickly to be seen clearly if the computer were allowed simply to make the calculation and display it. To slow the computer down, a delay loop is added at lines 340 and 350. These commands in effect tell the computer to count to 500 before doing anything else. To make the display run more quickly, decrease the figure in the delay. Line 370 instructs the computer to go back to line 330, display the figure obtained for height and run through to obtain a new value for height. This is repeated until the value obtained for height is greater than the target set for achieving orbit.

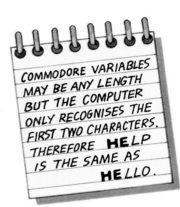

COMMODORE VARIABLES MAY BE ANY LENGTH BUT THE COMPUTER ONLY RECOGNISES THE FIRST TWO CHARACTERS. THEREFORE **HELP** IS THE SAME AS **HE**LLO.

```
380 PRINT CHR$(147)
390 FOR RO= 1 TO 15
400 PRINT SPC(11);"SHUTTLE IN ORBIT !!!!"
410 NEXT RO
420 PRINT "██   CONGRATULATIONS CAPTAIN ";NA$
```

The final section of the program displays the congratulatory message. It uses a **FOR......NEXT** loop in lines 390 to 410 as an easy way of printing SHUTTLE IN ORBIT 15 times. It works by using **RO** (short for row) as its loop variable, in this case having values ranging from 1 to 15. In effect, it tells the computer to print on each screen row from row 1 to row 15. Without this loop, it would be necessary to copy line 400 fifteen times, with a different program line for each row of the display.

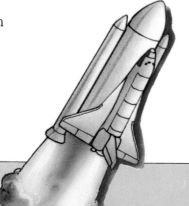

Improve your program

One of the best ways of learning about programming is to experiment with the programs you type in. Try deleting the delay in lines 340 and 350 and see what happens. Change the number of guesses the player is allowed by altering lines 180 and 250. Always keep a note of the changes you make, so that you can restore the program to its original form when you want to.

 Adding sound

APPLE IIe

The addition of sound to your program will make the game more exciting. However, the instructions for obtaining complex sounds are too complicated to be explained here. The simple **FOR. . . . .NEXT** loop given below will give sounds as the shuttle takes off. The **PEEK** command in line 345 tells the computer to look into that part of the memory where sounds are controlled. The **FOR. . . . .NEXT** loop instructs the computer to do this fifty times before going on to the next stage of the program.

```
340   FOR SOUND = 1 TO 50
345   LET S =  PEEK ( - 16336)
350   NEXT SOUND
```

COMMODORE 64

The Commodore can produce extremely interesting sounds, but the programming commands needed are very complex. Sound is available by using the **POKE** instruction, followed by two sets of figures. The **POKE** instruction is beyond the scope of this book, but try these additions to your program to add sounds to the liftoff display:

```
365 POKE54277,15:POKE54278,81:POKE54296,15:
    POKE54276,129
366 POKE54273,HI/65:FORT=0TO60:NEXT
375 POKE54276,128
```

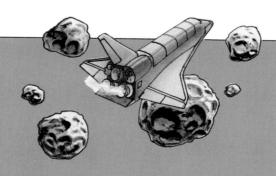

ASTEROIDS

The shuttle is successfully in orbit. Suddenly, you run into a freak asteroid storm. You must give the shuttle's computer flight directions in order to pilot your craft safely through the storm. There's no going back, and a collision means certain destruction for you and your ship.

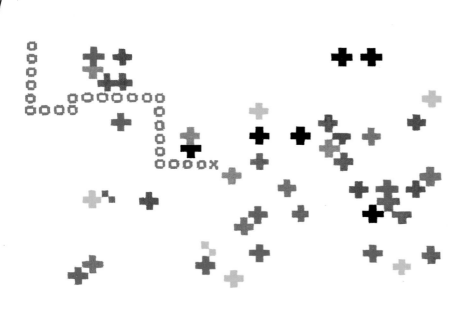

This program displays asteroids and the shuttle on the screen, and enables the shuttle to move in the direction the player wants. In line 10, **GR** sets the computer to low resolution graphics mode, and **HOME** clears the screen.

```
5    REM   ASTEROIDS
10   GR  :  HOME
```

The first section of the program draws the asteroids at random positions on the screen, so that there are different asteroid positions each time the game is played.

Before the asteroids' positions are actually plotted, you should plan how you want the screen to look. In **GR** mode there is space for four lines of text at the bottom of the screen. The graphics area is a grid with 40 vertical coordinates and 40 horizontal coordinates, each numbered from 0 to 39. The top left-hand corner of the screen has the coordinates 0, 0. Logically, the shuttle should begin its journey at the left-hand side of the screen – vertical column 0. The asteroid field will extend from column 2 to column 36 and the shuttle will have reached its objective if it gets past column 37 without hitting an asteroid. In addition, the shuttle should not be able to fly off the bottom of the screen to avoid the asteroids. Taken together, these considerations will produce the screen plan shown in the illustration below. You could have a different plan, in which case you'll have to change the figures in the **VTAB** and **HTAB** instructions of the program that plot screen positions accordingly.

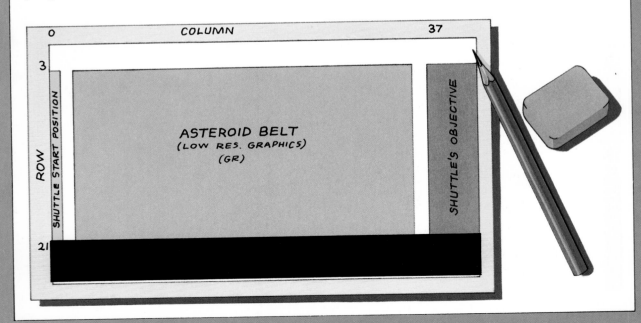

```
20    DIM AC(40),DO(40)
30    FOR AS = 1 TO 40

40    LET AC(AS) =   INT ( RND (1) * 35) + 2
50    LET DO(AS) =   INT ( RND (1) * 38) + 1
60    COLOR= 5
61    PLOT AC(AS),DO(AS) - 1: PLOT AC(AS) - 1,DO(AS)
62    PLOT AC(AS),DO(AS): PLOT AC(AS) + 1,DO(AS)
63    PLOT AC(AS),DO(AS) + 1
70    NEXT AS
```

In line 20, the **DIM** command opens two *arrays* in which the
positions of the asteroids **AC**ross and **DO**wn the screen are
stored. The number in brackets which follows indicates the
number of asteroids – 40 gives a good display. Lines 40 and
50 generate random row and column positions for the
asteroids within the limits set for the display. Line 60 sets
COLOR to **5** which gives graphics colored gray – until
COLOR is changed, everything **PLOT**ed is in gray. The
asteroid is actually built by lines 61, 62 and 63. Note that the
asteroid shape is made up of five blocks. **AC(AS),DO(AS)** is
the central position of the asteroid: line 61 **PLOT**s the block
of color directly below, and the block directly behind this
position. Line 62 **PLOT**s the central and the forward blocks,
and line 63 **PLOT**s the block above. The notepad shows
how each asteroid is built up from these **PLOT** instructions.

EACH ASTEROID IS CONSTRUCTED LIKE THIS:

	AC,DO+1	
AC-1,DO	AC,DO	AC+1,DO
	AC,DO-1	

Lines 40 to 63 have generated a random position and plotted
an asteroid there. The **FOR......NEXT** loop of lines 30 and 70
do this for all forty asteroids in turn.

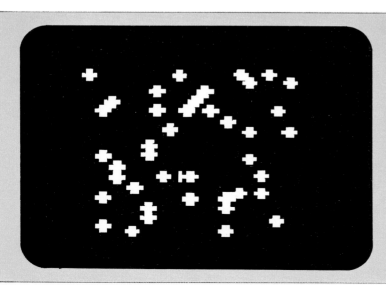

RUN

AFTER LINE **70** TYPE **RUN**
AND THE ASTEROID FIELD
SHOULD APPEAR ON YOUR
SCREEN.
IF YOU GET AN ERROR
MESSAGE CHECK BACK
THROUGH THE PROGRAM
LISTING.

```
100    LET CO = 0: LET RO =   INT ( RND (1) * 38) + 1
110    COLOR= 15
120    PLOT CO,RO
```

In line 100, the horizontal starting position (**CO** – short for column) of the shuttle is set at 0: the vertical position (**RO** – short for row) is chosen by generating a random number between 0 and 1 using **RND(1)**. This is multiplied by 38 and made a whole number using the **INT** statement. One is added so that the value of **RO** can never be zero. **COLOR** is reset to **15** in line 110, ready to **PLOT** the shuttle in white at the coordinates **CO,RO** in line 120.

Lines 160 to 220 enable the player to give the shuttle instructions for its journey through the asteroids. Three directions are enough – up, down and right – since the shuttle is moving from left to right across the screen. The direction is given by pressing the U, D, and R keys respectively. The **INPUT** is stored in the string variable **DI$**. If a key other than U, D, or R is pressed, then line 200 sends the program back to 160 for a correct input. The shuttle's direction is changed by changing the values of **UP** and **RI** in lines 170 to 190. Line 210 asks for distance that the shuttle is to travel in this new direction to be **INPUT**. Notice that there is no **$** sign since the input will be given in figures. Line 220 gives a different color to represent the shuttle's course, to distinguish it from the shuttle's current position.

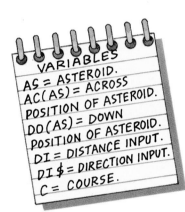

VARIABLES
AS = ASTEROID.
AC(AS) = ACROSS POSITION OF ASTEROID.
DO(AS) = DOWN POSITION OF ASTEROID.
DI = DISTANCE INPUT.
DI$ = DIRECTION INPUT.
C = COURSE.

```
160    VTAB 22: HTAB 1: INPUT "DIRECTION (UP,DOWN,
       RIGHT)";DI$
170    IF DI$ = "U" THEN UP =  - 1:RI = 0: GOTO 210
180    IF DI$ = "D" THEN UP = 1:RI = 0: GOTO 210
190    IF DI$ = "R" THEN UP = 0:RI = 1: GOTO 210
200    GOTO 160
210    INPUT "DISTANCE";DI
220    COLOR= 12: PLOT CO,RO
```

UP REPRESENTS THE VERTICAL MOTION.
RIGHT IS THE HORIZONTAL MOTION.

UP-1 ("U")
RIGHT +1 ("R")
UP+1 ("D")

Lines 230 to 330 might be thought of as the heart of the program. They allow the shuttle to be piloted across the screen by the player and check that no collisions with any of the asteroids have occurred. This whole section is contained within a **FOR......NEXT** loop which uses **C** (short for course) as its variable. This loop is repeated for as many times as the figure for distance input at line 210. What happens is that the shuttle's new position is found using **UP** and **RI** in lines 240 and 250. The shuttle moves to these new column and row coordinates one unit at a time. The lines that follow check each new position for success or failure.

THE SHUTTLE'S PATH IS A GREEN RECTANGLE.

THE SHUTTLE'S POSITION IS A WHITE RECTANGLE.

```
230   FOR C = 1 TO DI
240   LET RO = RO + UP
250   LET CO = CO + RI
260   FOR AS = 1 TO 40
270   IF CO = AC(AS) AND (RO = DO(AS) - 1 OR
      RO = DO(AS) + 1) THEN  GOTO 370
280   IF RO = DO(AS) AND (CO = AC(AS) - 1 OR
      CO = AC(AS) + 1) THEN  GOTO 370
290   NEXT AS
300   IF RO > 39 OR RO < 1 THEN  GOTO 390
310   COLOR= 12: PLOT CO,RO
320.  IF CO > 37 THEN  GOTO 410
330   NEXT C
340   GOTO 110
```

In lines 260 to 290 another **FOR......NEXT** loop is used to check to see if the shuttle has collided with an asteroid. The actual coordinates for an asteroid stored in the array in line 20 are for the center of the asteroid. The positions plotted on the screen also include the coordinates above, below and to the right and left of this position. So lines 270 and 280 compare the shuttle's coordinates with these coordinates, since the shuttle will collide with these first. The loop does this for all 40 asteroids in turn. Line 300 checks to see if the new position takes the shuttle "out of orbit." If all is well, the new position for the shuttle is plotted by line 310. The final check is to see if the shuttle has reached column 38 safely. Lastly, line 340 sends the program back to line 110 for the next course and distance to be input.

CRASH

MISS, NEXT ASTEROID

MISS, NEXT ASTEROID

MISS, NEXT ASTEROID

MISS, NEXT ASTEROID

All that remains to do is to add the final messages for success or failure in the game – "YOU HAVE CRASHED INTO AN ASTEROID AND YOUR SHIP IS TERMINALLY DAMAGED!!!" and so on. The **HTAB** and **VTAB** instructions and the placing of the message on two lines simply give a better screen display. There are three end messages – one for collision with an asteroid, one for going out of orbit and one for success.

```
370   HOME : VTAB 21: HTAB 5: PRINT "YOU HAVE CRASHED
      INTO AN ASTEROID"
380   VTAB 22: HTAB 5: PRINT "AND YOUR SHIP IS
      TERMINALLY DAMAGED": END
390   HOME : VTAB 21: HTAB 5: PRINT "YOU HAVE GONE OUT
      OF ORBIT"
400   VTAB 22: HTAB 5: PRINT "AND ARE LOST IN SPACE":
      END
410   HOME : VTAB 21: HTAB 5: PRINT "WELL DONE! YOU
      MISSED THEM ALL!"
420   VTAB 22: HTAB 5: PRINT "YOU QUALIFY AS A SHUTTLE
      PILOT"
430   END
```

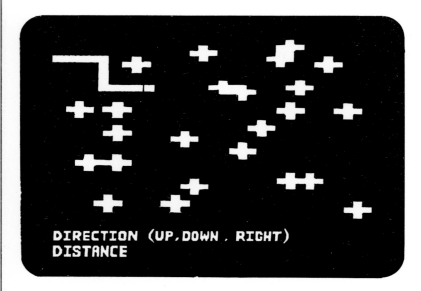

```
DIRECTION (UP,DOWN , RIGHT)
DISTANCE
```

Don't forget to add the **END** instruction at the end of lines 380 and 400 – if you leave them out the computer will always run through to the final lines of program, and you would receive the congratulations message each time you played the game. **STOP** has the same effect, but if you use this the computer would report **"BREAK IN 380"** when the shuttle collided with an asteroid, for example.

This program uses some of the block graphics available from the Commodore 64. It displays the asteroids and the shuttle on the screen and enables the shuttle to be moved according to the commands input during the game. As before, a **REM** statement gives the program its title and the screen is cleared using **PRINT CHR$(147)**.

```
5 REM  ASTEROIDS
10 PRINT CHR$(147)
```

The first thing to do, before writing the section of program for drawing the asteroids at random positions on the screen, is to plan how the screen should look. The Commodore 64 has a screen width of 40 columns and a depth of 25 rows, numbered 0 to 39 and 0 to 24 respectively. The shuttle should travel from left to right across the screen, so its logical starting point should be in column 0. The asteroid field should occupy most of the screen – in this case it extends from column 3 to column 32. The shuttle will have reached its objective when it gets past column 33 without colliding with an asteroid. The top three rows of the screen should be reserved to display instructions for piloting the shuttle, progress messages and allow inputs to be given during the course of the game. In addition, the shuttle should not be able to fly off the top or bottom of the screen to avoid the asteroid field. Taken together, these considerations will produce the screen plan shown below. You could work out a different design for the game, but if you do so, you'll have to change some of the figures in the **PRINT** instructions.

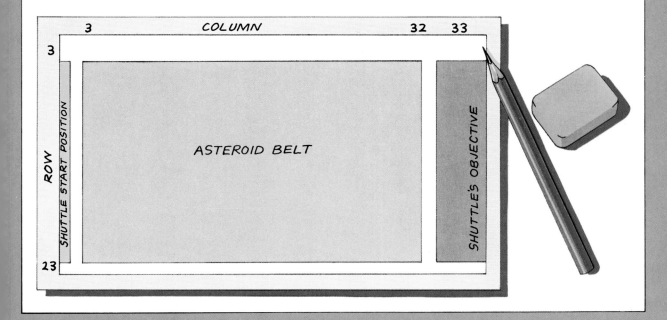

```
20 DIM AC(50) , DO(50)
25 UD$="▚□□□□□□□□□□□□□□□□□□□□□"
30 FOR AS=1 TO 50
40 AC(AS)=INT(RND(0)*30)+3
50 DO(AS)=INT(RND(0)*20)+4
60 PRINT LEFT$(UD$,DO(AS))SPC(AC(AS))"∎"
65 PRINT LEFT$(UD$,DO(AS)+1)SPC(AC(AS))"▚ ▰ "
70 NEXT AS
```

In line 20, the **DIM** command opens two *arrays* in which the positions of the asteroids across and down the screen are stored. The number following in brackets indicates the number of asteroids and hence the size of the array required. Line 25 uses **UD$** to store a string of cursor control codes. These are used later to move the cursor to the desired position down the screen for printing, as in line 110. Lines 30 to 70 are a **FOR......NEXT** loop which allow the commands contained in lines 40 to 65 to be performed for each of the 50 asteroids in turn. The loop variable **AS** stands for asteroid. Lines 40 to 50 generate random column and row numbers which plot the position of each asteroid on the screen. Line 60 produces the top part of the asteroid using the graphics symbol on the "D" Key. To get the symbol, press the Commodore logo key and "D" together. Line 65 gives the bottom part, made from two characters. The first character is reversed – the symbol in the listing is the exact opposite of what appears on the screen. See the notepad opposite on how to obtain reversed characters. The second character is obtained by pressing the Commodore logo key and "V" together. **RUN** this section as shown below.

LOWER SECTION OF ASTEROID
TO PRODUCE ▜
TYPE...
SP(AC(AS)) ⬛▜—⬛
REVERSE ON REVERSE OFF
THE 'REVERSE ON' SYMBOL "⬛"
IS 'CTRL' WITH "9"
THE REVERSE OFF "⬛" IS
'CTRL' WITH "∅"

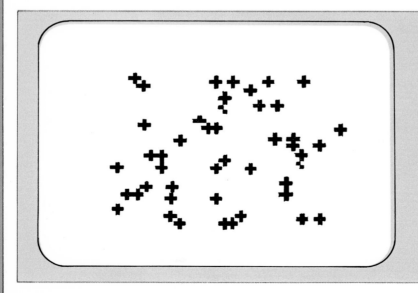

RUN

AFTER LINE 70 TYPE RUN AND THE ASTEROID FIELD SHOULD APPEAR ON YOUR SCREEN. IF YOU GET AN ERROR MESSAGE CHECK BACK THROUGH THE PROGRAM LISTING.

```
80  TI$="000000"
90  C$="                                      "
100 CO=0: RO=INT(RND(0)*20)+4
110 PRINT LEFT$(UD$,RO)SPC(CO)"X"
120 PRINT "⊠"C$
130 PRINT C$
140 PRINT "⊠TIME TAKEN:"MID$(TI$,3,2)" MINUTES :";
145 PRINT RIGHT$(TI$,2)" SECONDS"
150 IF VAL(MID$(TI$,4,1))>2 THEN 350
```

In line 80 **TI$**, the time, is set at zero and has six characters.
The first two characters count hours, the second two,
minutes, and the third, seconds. In line 140, the **MID$**
command takes the third and fourth characters to display the
minutes and in 145, **RIGHT$** takes the last two characters of
TI$ to display the seconds. Line 150 takes the program to
line 350 where the run out of time message is displayed if the
VALue of the fourth character is greater than 2 – that is,
when two minutes have elapsed. The string of 38 spaces
stored in line 90 is used in lines 120 and 130 to overprint the
old values displayed at the top of the screen. Lines 100 and
110 **PRINT** an "X" at a random position in column 0, to
represent the shuttle ready to begin its journey.

```
160 INPUT "DIRECTION (UP,DOWN, RIGHT)";DI$
170 IF DI$="U" THEN UP=-1:RI=0:GOTO 210
180 IF DI$="D" THEN UP=1:RI=0:GOTO 210
190 IF DI$="R" THEN UP=0:RI=1:GOTO 210
200 GOTO 120
210 INPUT "DISTANCE";DI
220 PRINT LEFT$(UD$,RO)SPC(CO)"0"
```

Lines 160 to 220 allow the shuttle to be given course and
distance instructions for its flight. Three directions – up,
down and right – are enough, since the shuttle is moving
from left to right across the screen. The direction is **INPUT**
using the U, D and R keys respectively. The **INPUT** is stored
under the string variable **DI$**. If an incorrect key is pressed,
line 200 sends the program back to 120 until one of the valid
keys is pressed. In line 220 the shuttle symbol will be
changed to a "0" to represent its path.

SHUTTLE'S PATH

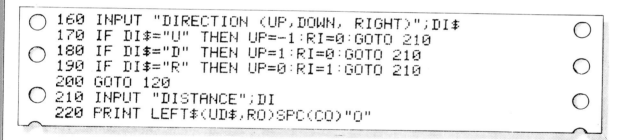

SHUTTLE'S PATH   SHUTTLE'S POSITION

Lines 170 to 190 set the values for the change in the shuttle's course, by using **UP** to set the change in direction up or down, and **RI** to direct the shuttle to move to the right. The actual change in the shuttle's position only takes place after the distance has been input. This input is allowed by line 210. Notice that a string variable sign isn't needed for this **INPUT** because the distance given will be given in figures. Finally in this section, the shuttle symbol is changed from an X into a 0 so that the shuttle's path through the asteroids and the shuttle's current position don't get confused.

VARIABLES

AS = ASTEROID.
AC(AS) = ACROSS POSITION OF ASTEROID.
DO(AS) = DOWN.
DI$ = DIRECTION INPUT.
DI = DISTANCE INPUT.
C = COURSE.

Lines 230 to 330 are really the heart of the program. They cause the shuttle to move across the screen and check that no collisions have occurred. This whole section is contained within a **FOR......NEXT** loop which uses **C** (standing for course) as its variable. The loop is repeated for as many times as the figure for distance input in line 210. What happens is that the shuttle's new position is found in lines 240 and 250, using the values of **UP** and **RI** set in the previous section of the program. The shuttle moves to these new row and column coordinates one unit at a time.

```
230 FOR C=1 TO DI
240 RO=RO+UP
250 CO=CO+RI
260 FOR AS=1 TO 50
270 IF CO=AC(AS) AND RO=DO(AS) THEN 370
280 IF CO=AC(AS) AND RO=DO(AS)+1 THEN 370
285 IF CO=AC(AS)+1 AND RO=DO(AS)+1 THEN 370
290 NEXT AS
300 IF RO>24 OR RO<4 THEN 390
310 PRINT LEFT$(UD$,RO)SPC(CO)"0"
320 IF CO>33 THEN 410
330 NEXT C
340 GOTO 110
```

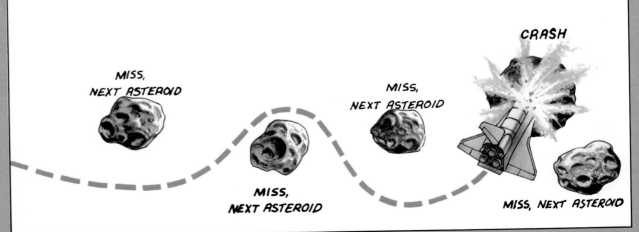

MISS, NEXT ASTEROID

MISS, NEXT ASTEROID

MISS, NEXT ASTEROID

CRASH

MISS, NEXT ASTEROID

In lines 260 to 290 another **FOR......NEXT** loop is used to check to see if the shuttle has collided with an asteroid. Lines 270 to 285 take the column and row positions of the shuttle and compare them with those for the asteroids stored in the array opened at line 20. Line 270 checks for collision with the graphics characters printed by line 60, and lines 280 and 285 check for the two characters printed by line 65. The loop does this for each asteroid in turn. Line 300 checks to see if the shuttle has gone out of orbit. If all is well, the shuttle is printed at the new position. The final check is to see if the shuttle has reached column 34. Lastly, line 340 sends the program back to 110 to ask for the next course and distance.

All that remains is to add the end messages. The cursor control codes and the placing of the messages on two lines simply give a better screen display. The reversed heart symbol before each message is the cursor control code for clearing the screen – it does the same as **CHR$(147)**.

```
350 PRINT "◧◧◧◧◧◧◧◧◧◧◧        YOU HAVE RUN OUT OF
    FUEL"
360 PRINT "◧◧       AND WILL DRIFT IN SPACE FOR EVER"
    :STOP
370 PRINT "◧◧◧◧◧◧◧◧◧◧◧◧   YOU HAVE CRASHED INTO AN
    ASTEROID"
380 PRINT "◧◧  AND YOUR SHIP IS TERMINALLY DAMAGED"
    :STOP
390 PRINT "◧◧◧◧◧◧◧◧◧◧◧◧        YOU HAVE GONE OUT OF
    ORBIT"
400 PRINT "◧◧       AND ARE LOST IN SPACE":STOP
410 PRINT "◧◧◧◧◧◧◧◧◧◧◧◧     WELL DONE! YOU MISSED THEM
    ALL!"
420 PRINT "◧◧     YOU QUALIFY AS A SHUTTLE PILOT":STOP
```

When you play the game, you should keep in mind how the asteroids are made up. They are composed of three graphics characters. The graphics characters used are made up from a combination of three blocks as shown in the diagram below. If the shuttle occupies any of the three blocks of any of the three graphics characters, then the computer will report a collision.

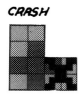

MISS

CRASH

CRASH

CRASH

Improve your program

You can make the game harder to play by increasing the number of asteroids, but after 120 or so, it is almost impossible to find a route through. Change lines 20, 30 and 260.

Adding colour

APPLE IIe

In **GR** mode, there are a total of sixteen colors available on the Apple IIe, obtained using the **COLOR** instruction followed by a number from 0 to 15. By using the **RND** command to generate a random number in this range, the asteroids can be randomly colored. Add the line below to achieve this. Notice that 1 is added to the random number – this is to ensure that the **COLOR** figure can never be zero which would produce a black asteroid, invisible against the black screen background.

```
60   COLOR=   INT ( RND (1) * 7) + 1
```

COMMODORE 64

To produce random colored asteroids for the Commodore, the **POKE** command must be used. 646 is the "address" for the area in the computer's memory which selects the printing color. The second figure in the **POKE** command gives the color selected. The section of program below chooses a random number between 1 and 8 to give randomly colored asteroids. This figure is not allowed to be six, as this is the color of the background and would produce an "invisible" asteroid.

```
55 XX=INT(RND(0)*8)+1:IFXX=6THEN55
60 POKE646,XX:PRINT LEFT$(UD$,DO(AS))SPC(AC(AS))" ∎"
```

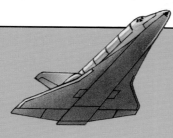

SHUTTLE LANDING

Because of the asteroid storm, your mission has been cut short and you must return to base. The landing point is in sight, but the shuttle's autopilot has malfunctioned. You must bring the shuttle safely to land using your manual controls. Key "A" increases your rate of descent and "D" decreases it. Your instrument panel will give you details of your flight path.

HEIGHT	DESCENT	SPEED	DISTANCE
1200	5	400	11600

Once again, the shuttle will travel from left to right across the graphics screen. The bottom four text lines are used to display the instrument panel, showing the shuttle's height, rate of descent, speed, and distance from the runway, and their respective values. The shuttle's objective, the runway, is represented by a blue block in the bottom right-hand corner of the screen. The shuttle and the runway are produced using **PLOT** statements. Once again, graphics mode is selected and the screen is cleared. The layout generated by the first lines will look like this:

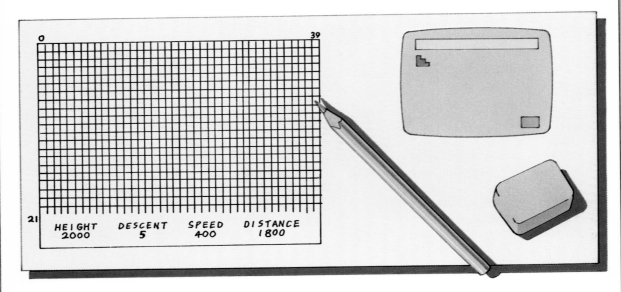

```
 5    REM   SHUTTLE LANDING
10    GR : HOME
20    LET D = 18000: LET S = 400: LET H = 2000:
      LET F = 5
30    LET C$ = "        "
40    VTAB 21: HTAB 2: PRINT "HEIGHT    DESCENT    SPEED
      DISTANCE"
50    COLOR= 2: PLOT 35,39: PLOT 36,39: PLOT 37,39:
      PLOT 38,39
```

Line 20 sets the initial values for the shuttle's distance from the runway, speed, height and rate of descent. The **VTAB** and **HTAB** instructions are used to position the instrument panel display – remember to include the three spaces between each heading. Line 30 stores a string of five spaces that will be used to overprint the old values on the instrument panel while the program is running. In line 50, **COLOR 2** gives a blue runway, made up of four graphics blocks, positioned by the **PLOT** statement on the 39th row of the graphics screen.

```
60    LET X = 0: LET Y = 1
70    COLOR= 1: PLOT X,Y: PLOT X + 1,Y: PLOT X,Y - 1
```

The shuttle's starting position on the screen is given by the coordinates X and Y in line 60, representing column and row positions across and down the screen which will be used to **PLOT** the shuttle later in the program. The shuttle is represented by the three blocks at positions **X, Y: X+1, Y** and **X, Y-1**, colored green by **COLOR 1.**

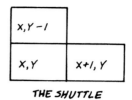

THE SHUTTLE

```
80    VTAB 22: HTAB 3: PRINT C$;
90    HTAB 3: PRINT H;
100   HTAB 13: PRINT C$;
110   HTAB 13: PRINT F;
120   HTAB 22: PRINT C$;
130   HTAB 22: PRINT S;
140   HTAB 30: PRINT C$;
150   HTAB 30: PRINT D;
```

Lines 80 to 150 display the figures for height, rate of descent, speed and distance from the runway, using **VTAB** and **HTAB** instructions to place them under the appropriate instrument panel display. The string variable, **C\$**, in lines 100, 120 and 140 contains the series of five spaces stored in line 30 and is used to blank out the old values of the figures on the instrument panel before they are updated later in the program, giving the impression of a running display as the shuttle is piloted down to the runway.

```
160   IF S < 200 THEN  HOME : VTAB 21: HTAB 10:
      PRINT "SHUTTLE STALLED": END
170   IF D <  - 800 THEN  HOME : VTAB 21: HTAB 5:
      PRINT "SHUTTLE HAS OVERSHOT RUNWAY": END
180   IF H <  = 0 THEN  GOTO 290
```

Lines 160 to 180 check the values for the shuttle's speed, distance and height to see if they agree with the conditions placed on the game. Line 160 checks that the speed hasn't dropped below 200, and clears the screen and prints the appropriate message if it has. Line 170 checks that the shuttle has not overshot the runway. In line 180, the program goes to line 290 if the shuttle has reached the landing height of zero. At line 290, another check will be made to see if the shuttle has landed close enough to the runway – within a distance of 1000 from the runway.

```
190    GET R$
200    IF R$ = "A" OR R$ = "a" THEN F = F + 1
       S = S + 5
210    IF R$ = "D" OR R$ = "d" THEN F = F - 1
       S = S - 5
220    IF F = 0 THEN F = 1:S = S - 20
225    IF F > 10 THEN F = 10
230    LET H = H - F: LET S = S + (F - 5) * 3:
       LET D = D -   INT (S / 10)
240    COLOR= 0: PLOT X,Y: PLOT X + 1,Y: PLOT X,Y - 1
250    LET X = 36 -   INT (D / (18000 / 36))
260    LET Y = 38 -   INT (H / (2000 / 38))
270    COLOR= 1: PLOT X,Y: PLOT X + 1,Y: PLOT X,Y - 1
280    GOTO 80
```

Lines 190 to 280 allows the player to control the shuttle's descent. At line 190, the **GET R$** command tells the computer to go to the keyboard to see if a key has been pressed. Any key that is pressed is stored in the **R$** – the program will wait until a key is pressed. Lines 200 and 210 check to see if **R$** was A or D (A increases the rate of descent, D decreases it). If any other key is pressed the rate of descent remains the same – use the S key to do this when you play the game. Lines 220 and 225 limit the rate of descent to a minimum value of one and a maximum of ten. Line 230 calculates new values for the shuttle's instrument panel, and line 240 prints the shuttle in the old position, colored black by **COLOR 0**. This effectively blanks out the shuttle. The shuttle's new position is calculated by lines 250 and 260 and printed by line 270.

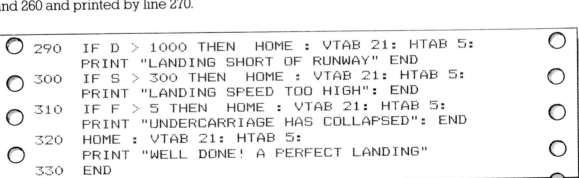

THE VALUES OF X AND Y IN LINES 250 AND 260 WILL BE SUCH THAT THE SHUTTLE IS NEVER PRINTED OFF THE SCREEN.

```
290    IF D > 1000 THEN   HOME : VTAB 21: HTAB 5:
       PRINT "LANDING SHORT OF RUNWAY" END
300    IF S > 300 THEN   HOME : VTAB 21: HTAB 5:
       PRINT "LANDING SPEED TOO HIGH": END
310    IF F > 5 THEN   HOME : VTAB 21: HTAB 5:
       PRINT "UNDERCARRIAGE HAS COLLAPSED": END
320    HOME : VTAB 21: HTAB 5:
       PRINT "WELL DONE! A PERFECT LANDING"
330    END
```

The final lines check that the landing is not short of the runway, or that the shuttle's speed or rate of descent is not too high. If not, the program runs to line 320 for the congratulations message.

As in the previous program, the first stage of preparation is to plan how the screen should look. Once again, the shuttle will travel from left to right across the screen, starting from the top left-hand corner. The shuttle's objective, the runway, is represented by a block in the bottom right-hand corner. The top of the screen is reserved to show the shuttle's instrument panel, displaying the shuttle's height, rate of descent, speed and distance from the runway. These considerations result in a screen layout like the one shown in the illustration below.

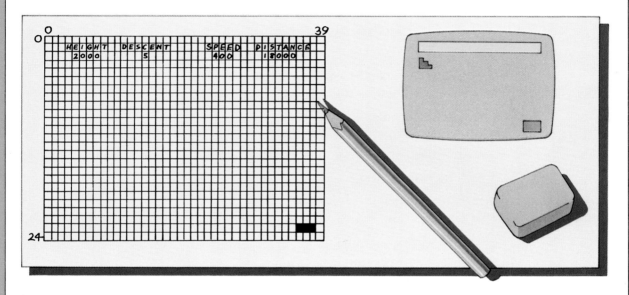

```
5 REM SHUTTLE LANDING
10 PRINT"⊐"
20 D=18000:S=400:H=2000:F=5
30 C$="      "
35 UD$="◆◖◖◖◖◖◖◖◖◖◖◖◖◖◖◖◖◖◖◖◖◖◖◖◖"
40 PRINT"◼   HEIGHT  ◣DESCENT  ▦SPEED  ◼DISTANCE"
50 PRINTLEFT$(UD$,24)SPC(35)"◼◰    "
```

Line 20 sets the initial values for the speed, height, rate of descent, and distance from the runway for the shuttle. At line 30, a string of six spaces is stored in **C$**, to be used later to overprint the instrument panel. Line 35 stores a set of cursor control codes, used to position the display later in the program. The instrument panel is printed by line 40. Color text is available directly from the keyboard by pressing either the control or the Commodore logo key together with the numbers 1-8. For example, light red is given by the logo key with 3. In the program these colors are represented by color codes in lines 40 and 50. The code in line 50 colors the landing pad light green.

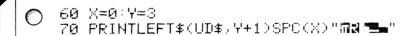
```
60 X=0:Y=3
70 PRINTLEFT$(UD$,Y+1)SPC(X)"▓▓ ▀▄"
```

The shuttle's starting position at the top of the screen is given
by the coordinates X and Y in line 60. The shuttle is printed
yellow, using the reverse on and off codes, similar to those
used to print an asteroid in the last program. The shuttle's tail
is made using the logo key and "C", and the body is given by
using the Commodore logo key with "I".

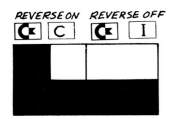

```
80  PRINT"▓▓▓    "C$
90  PRINT"▓▓▓▓    "H
100 PRINT"▓▓▓"SPC(13)C$
110 PRINT"▄▓▓▓"SPC(13)F
120 PRINT"▓▓▓"SPC(20)C$
130 PRINT"▓▓▓▓"SPC(20)S
140 PRINT"▓▓▓"SPC(27)C$
150 PRINT"■▓▓▓"SPC(27)D
```

Lines 80 to 150 display the figures for speed, rate of descent,
height, and distance from the runway, placed under the
appropriate headings on the instrument panel. Again, the
same color control codes produce a colored display. The
string variable **C$** in lines 80, 100, 120 and 140 uses the string
of six spaces stored in line 30 to blank out the old values
displayed before they are updated. This will give the
impression of a running display on the instrument panel as
the shuttle moves downward across the screen towards the
landing pad.

```
160 IF S<200 THEN PRINT LEFT$(UD$,11)SPC(12)"▄SHUTTLE
    STALLED":STOP
170 IF D<-999 THEN PRINT LEFT$(UD$,11)"▄  SHUTTLE HAS
    OVERSHOT THE RUNWAY":STOP
180 IF H<=0 THEN 290
```

Lines 160 to 180 check that the speed is not too low and that
the shuttle has not overshot the runway by more than the
figure of 999. Line 180 checks to see if the shuttle has
reached the landing height of zero. If so, the program goes to
line 290, where a final check will be made to see if the
landing has met the other conditions necessary for success.
The **LEFT$(UD$, 11)** instruction uses part of the string of
cursor control codes stores in line 35 to position the
messages down the screen.

```
190 GETR$
200 IF R$="A" THEN F=F+1:S=S+5
210 IF R$="D" THEN F=F-1:S=S-5
220 IF F=0 THEN F=1:S=S-20
230 H=H-F:S=S+(F-5)*3:D=D-INT(S/10)
240 PRINT LEFT$(UD$,Y+1)SPC(X)C$
250 X=35-INT(D/(18000/35))
260 Y=22-INT(H/(2000/19))
270 PRINT LEFT$(UD$,Y+1)SPC(X)"▇▇ ▆▆"
280 GOTO80
```

From line 190 to 280, the program allows the player to control
the shuttle's descent. At line 190, the **GET R$** command tells
the computer to go to the keyboard to see if a key has been
pressed. Any key that is pressed is stored in the variable **R$**.
Lines 200 and 210 check to see if the key stored in **R$** is an A
or a D (standing for accelerate and decelerate respectively).
If so, the descent and speed values are changed
accordingly. At line 220, the program ensures that the rate of
descent can never be zero – if it were, the shuttle would stop
altogether. Line 230 calculates the new values of height,
speed and distance to be displayed on the instrument panel.
In line 240, part of the cursor control codes stored in **UD$** is
used to position the cursor appropriately, and the spaces
stored in **C$** are used to overprint the old position of the
shuttle. The new positions of the X and Y coordinates for the
shuttle are calculated in lines 250 and 260, using the new
values of height and distance. Line 270 prints the shuttle at
this new position, and at 280 the program returns to line 80 to
continue the shuttle's descent.

THE VALUES OF X
AND Y IN LINES
250 AND 260 WILL
BE SUCH THAT
THE SHUTTLE IS
NEVER PRINTED
OFF THE SCREEN.

```
290 IF D>1000 THEN PRINT LEFT$(UD$,11)"▇     LANDING
       SHORT OF RUNWAY":STOP
300 IF S>300 THEN PRINT LEFT$(UD$,11)"▇     LANDING
    SPEED TOO HIGH":STOP
310 IF F>5 THEN PRINT LEFT$(UD$,11)
    "▇     UNDERCARRIAGE COLLAPSED":STOP
320 PRINT LEFT$(UD$,11)"▇    WELL DONE, A PERFECT
    LANDING!!!":STOP
```

Lastly come the end messages. These also check that the
landing is not short of the runway, nor the speed or rate of
descent too high. If all these conditions are met, then the
program runs through to line 320 and the congratulations
message is printed.

Improve your programs

The final improvement is to link all three games together. Other changes have been made in the listing below, and the lines are indicated by an asterisk. Before the linking can begin you must renumber the program lines in the second and third programs.

Linking the programs

APPLE IIe

To make the link, a *subroutine* is added at line 3000. This gives an "ALERT!!" display plus sounds. Line 440 and 1440 take the program to the subroutine at the end of each section. Lines 430 and 1430 give the appropriate word to appear in the display in each case.

COMMODORE 64

The Commodore linking subroutine is added at line 3000. It contains a short delay and then gives an "ALERT!!" display before the next section of the game begins. Lines 440 and 1440 call up the subroutine.

```
  5     REM   SHUTTLE LAUNCH
 10     TEXT : HOME
 20     VTAB 4: HTAB 13: PRINT "SHUTTLE LAUNCH"
 30     HTAB 13: PRINT "-------------"
 40     VTAB 8: HTAB 3: PRINT "THE SHUTTLE IS READY FOR
        LIFT OFF"
 50     VTAB 10: HTAB 3: PRINT "YOUR TASK IS TO LAUNCH
        IT"
 55     FLASH
 60     VTAB 13: HTAB 3: PRINT "YOU MAY ONLY HAVE TEN
        ATTEMPTS!!!"
 65     NORMAL
 70     VTAB 16: HTAB 3: PRINT "PLEASE ENTER YOUR NAME"
 80     VTAB 18: HTAB 3: PRINT "BY TYPING IT AND PRESSING
        RETURN"
 85     VTAB 20: HTAB 3
 90     INPUT NA$
100     HOME
110     HTAB 4: PRINT "WELCOME ABOARD, CAPTAIN ";NA$
120     VTAB 8: HTAB 5: PRINT "TO LAUNCH THE SHUTTLE YOU
        MUST"
130     VTAB 10: HTAB 5: PRINT "GUESS THE POWER LEVEL
        REQUIRED"
140     VTAB 12: HTAB 5: PRINT "(ANY NUMBER BETWEEN 1
        AND 100)"
150     VTAB 14: HTAB 5: PRINT "TYPE IT IN AND PRESS
        RETURN"
160     VTAB 16: HTAB 12: PRINT "GO AHEAD, PLEASE"
170     LET LEV =  INT ( RND (1) * 100 + 1
180     FOR A = 1 TO 10
185     FLASH : VTAB 18: HTAB 5: PRINT "ATTEMPT NUMBER "
        ;A: NORMAL
190     VTAB 19: HTAB 18: INPUT GU
200     IF GU = LEV THEN  GOTO 280
205     VTAB 21: HTAB 10
210     IF GU < LEV THEN  PRINT "TOO LOW, TRY AGAIN "
220     IF GU > LEV THEN  PRINT "TOO HIGH, TRY AGAIN"
230     NEXT A
240     HOME
250     VTAB 10: HTAB 2: PRINT "YOU HAVE FAILED AFTER
        TEN ATTEMPTS"
260     VTAB 12: HTAB 1: PRINT "TYPE 'RUN' AND PRESS
        RETURN TO TRY AGAIN"
270     STOP
280     HOME
290     LET HE = 0
300     LET TA = 10000
310     VTAB 5: HTAB 13: PRINT "LIFT-OFF!!!"
320     VTAB 10: HTAB 10: PRINT "HEIGHT"
330     VTAB 10: HTAB 20: PRINT HE
340     FOR SOUND = 1 TO 50
345     LET S =  PEEK ( - 16336)
350     NEXT SOUND
360     LET HE = HE * 2 + 1
370     IF HE < TA GOTO 330
380     HOME
390     FOR RO = 10 TO 15
400     VTAB RO: HTAB 11: PRINT "SHUTTLE IN ORBIT!!!!"
410     NEXT RO
420     VTAB 19: HTAB 2: PRINT "CONGRATULATIONS
        CAPTAIN ";NA$
*430     LET F$ = "ASTEROID "
*440     GOSUB 3000: REM  LINK
1000    REM   ASTEROIDS
1010    GR : HOME
```

```
  5 REM SHUTTLE LAUNCH
 10 PRINT CHR$(147)
 20 PRINT SPC(13);"SHUTTLE LAUNCH"
 30 PRINT SPC(13);"-------------"
 40 PRINT SPC(3);"THE SHUTTLE IS READY FOR LIFT-OFF"
 50 PRINT SPC(3);"YOUR TASK IS TO LAUNCH IT"
 60 PRINT SPC(3);"YOU MAY HAVE ONLY TEN ATTEMPTS
    !!!"
 70 PRINT SPC(3);"PLEASE ENTER YOUR NAME"
 80 PRINT SPC(3);"BY TYPING IT AND PRESSING RETURN"
 90 INPUT NA$
100 PRINT CHR$(147)
110 PRINT "WELCOME ABOARD,CAPTAIN ";NA$
120 PRINT SPC(5);"TO LAUNCH THE SHUTTLE YOU MUST"
130 PRINT SPC(5)"GUESS THE POWER LEVEL REQUIRED"
140 PRINT SPC(5)"(ANY NUMBER BETWEEN 1 AND 100)"
150 PRINT SPC(6)"TYPE IT IN AND PRESS RETURN"
160 PRINT SPC(12)"GO AHEAD,PLEASE"
170 LE=INT(RND(0)*100)
180 FOR AT=1 TO 10
185 PRINT ""SPC(11)" ATTEMPT
    NUMBER "AT""
190 INPUT "      ";GU
200 IF GU=LE THEN GOTO 280
210 IF GU<LE THEN PRINT SPC(7);GU;".. TOO LOW, TRY
    AGAIN"
220 IF GU>LE THEN PRINT SPC(7);GU;"..TOO HIGH, TRY
    AGAIN"
230 NEXT AT
240 PRINT CHR$(147)
250 PRINT SPC(2)"YOU HAVE FAILED AFTER TEN
    ATTEMPTS!!"
260 PRINT"TYPE 'RUN' AND PRESS RETURN TO TRY AGAIN"
270 STOP
280 PRINT CHR$(147)
290 HI=0
300 TA=10000
310 PRINT SPC(14);"LIFT-OFF!!!!"
320 PRINT SPC(16);"HEIGHT"
330 PRINT SPC(16);""HI
340 FOR DE=1 TO 500
350 NEXT DE
360 HI=HI*2+1
365 POKE54277,15:POKE54278,81:POKE54296,15:POKE54276
    ,129
367 POKE54273,HI/65:FORT=0TO60:NEXT
370 IF HI<TA THEN GOTO 330
375 POKE54276,128
380 PRINT CHR$(147)
390 FOR RO= 1 TO 15
400 PRINT SPC(11);"SHUTTLE IN ORBIT !!!!"
410 NEXT RO
420 PRINT "  CONGRATULATIONS CAPTAIN ";NA$
*430 F$="ASTEROID"
*440 GOSUB3000
1000 REM  ASTEROIDS
1010 PRINT CHR$(147)
1020 DIM AC(50) , DO(50)
1025 UD$="
1030 FOR AS=1 TO 50
1040 AC(AS)=INT(RND(0)*30)+3
1050 DO(AS)=INT(RND(0)*20)+4
1055 XX=INT(RND(0)*8)+1:IFXX=6THEN1055
1060 POKE646,XX:PRINT LEFT$(UD$,DO(AS))SPC(AC(AS))" ."
```

```
1020  DIM AC(40),DO(40)
1030  FOR AS = 1 TO 40
1040  LET AC(AS) =  INT ( RND (1) * 35) + 2
1050  LET DO(AS) =  INT ( RND (1) * 38) + 1
1060  COLOR=  INT ( RND (1) * 7) + 1
1061  PLOT AC(AS),DO(AS) - 1: PLOT AC(AS) - 1,DO(AS)
1062  PLOT AC(AS),DO(AS): PLOT AC(AS) + 1,DO(AS)
1063  PLOT AC(AS),DO(AS) + 1
1070  NEXT AS
1100  LET CO = 0: LET RO =  INT ( RND (1) * 38) + 1
1110  COLOR= 15
1120  PLOT CO,RO
1160  VTAB 22: HTAB 1: INPUT "DIRECTION(UP,DOWN,RIGHT)";DI$
1170  IF DI$ = "U" THEN UP =  - 1:RI = 0: GOTO 1210
1180  IF DI$ = "D" THEN UP = 1:RI = 0: GOTO 1210
1190  IF DI$ = "R" THEN UP = 0: RI = 1: GOTO 1210
1200  GOTO 1160
1210  INPUT "DISTANCE";DI
1220  COLOR= 12: PLOT CO,RO
1230  FOR C = 1 TO DI
1240  LET RO = RO + UP
1250  LET CO = CO + RI
1260  FOR AS = 1 TO 40
1270  IF CO = AC(AS) AND (RO = DO(AS) - 1 OR
      RO = DO(AS) + 1) THEN  GOTO 1370
1280  IF RO = DO(AS) AND (CO = AC(AS) - 1 OR
      CO = AC(AS) + 1) THEN  GOTO 1370
1290  NEXT AS
1300  IF RO > 39 OR RO < 1 THEN  GOTO 1390
1310  COLOR= 12: PLOT CO,RO
1320  IF CO > 37 THEN  GOTO 1410
1330  NEXT C
1340  GOTO 1110
1370  HOME : VTAB 21: HTAB 5: PRINT "YOU HAVE CRASHED
      INTO AN ASTEROID"
1380  VTAB 22: HTAB 5: PRINT "AND YOUR SHIP IS
      TERMINALLY DAMAGED": END
1390  HOME : VTAB 21: HTAB 5: PRINT "YOU HAVE GONE
      OUT OF ORBIT"
1400  VTAB 22: HTAB 5: PRINT "AND ARE LOST IN SPACE":
      END
1410  HOME : VTAB 21: HTAB 5: PRINT "WELL DONE! YOU
      MISSED THEM ALL!"
1420  VTAB 22: HTAB 5: PRINT "YOU QUALIFY AS A
      SHUTTLE PILOT"
1430  LET F$ = "LANDING "
1440  GOSUB 3000: REM  LINK
2000  REM  SHUTTLE LANDING
2010  GR : HOME
2020  LET D = 18000: LET S = 400: LET H = 2000:
      LET F = 5
2030  LET C$ = "        "
2040  VTAB 21: HTAB 2: PRINT "HEIGHT     DESCENT
      SPEED    DISTANCE"
2050  COLOR= 10: PLOT 35,39: PLOT 36,39: PLOT 37,39:
      PLOT 38,39
2060  LET X = 0: LET Y = 1
2070  COLOR= 15: PLOT X,Y: PLOT X + 1,Y: PLOT X,Y - 1
2080  VTAB 22: HTAB 3: PRINT C$;
2090  HTAB 3: PRINT H;
2100  HTAB 13: PRINT C$;
2110  HTAB 13: PRINT F;
2120  HTAB 22: PRINT C$;
2130  HTAB 22: PRINT S;
2140  HTAB 30: PRINT C$;
2150  HTAB 30: PRINT D;
2160  IF S < 200 THEN  HOME : VTAB 21: HTAB 10:
      PRINT "SHUTTLE STALLED": END
2170  IF D <  - 800 THEN  HOME : VTAB 21: HTAB 5:
      PRINT "SHUTTLE HAS OVERSHOT RUNWAY": END
2180  IF H <  = 0 THEN  GOTO 2300
2190  GET R$
2200  IF R$ = "A" OR R$ = "a" THEN F = F + 1:
      S = S + 5
2210  IF R$ = "D" OR R$ = "d" THEN F = F - 1:
      S = S - 5
2220  IF F = 0 THEN F = 1:S = S - 20
2225  IF F > 10 THEN F = 10
2230  LET H = H - F: LET S = S + (F - 5) * 3:
      LET D = D -  INT (S / 10)
2240  COLOR= 0: PLOT X,Y: PLOT X + 1,Y: PLOT X,Y - 1
2250  LET X = 36 -  INT (D / (18000 / 36))
2260  LET Y = 38 -  INT (H / (2000 / 38))
2270  COLOR= 15: PLOT X,Y: PLOT X + 1,Y: PLOT X,Y - 1
2280  GOTO 2080
2290  IF D > 1000 THEN  HOME : VTAB 21: HTAB 5:
      PRINT "LANDING SHORT OF RUNWAY": END
2300  IF S > 300 THEN  HOME : VTAB 21: HTAB 5:
      PRINT "LANDING SPEED TOO HIGH": END
2310  IF F > 5 THEN  HOME : VTAB 21: HTAB 5:
      PRINT "UNDERCARRIAGE HAS COLLAPSED": END
2320  HOME : VTAB 21: HTAB 5: PRINT "WELL DONE!
      A PERFECT LANDING!"
2330  END
3000  REM  LINK
3010  FOR BLEEP = 1 TO 20
3020  PRINT  CHR$ (7);
3030  NEXT BLEEP
3040  TEXT : HOME
3050  FOR LO = 1 TO 20
3060  VTAB LO: HTAB 1: PRINT "ALERT!!!";
      F$;"FIELD AHEAD!!!"
3070  NEXT LO
3080  FOR DE = 1 TO 3000
3090  NEXT DE
3100  RETURN
```

```
1065  PRINT LEFT$(UD$,DO(AS)+1)SPC(AC(AS))"◖▉◗"
1070  NEXT AS
1080  TI$="000000"
1090  C$="          "
1100  CO=0: RO=INT(RND(0)*20)+4
1110  PRINT LEFT$(UD$,RO)SPC(CO)"X"
1120  PRINT "▓"C$
1130  PRINT C$
1140  PRINT "▓TIME TAKEN:"MID$(TI$,3,2)" MINUTES :",
1145  PRINT RIGHT$(TI$,2)" SECONDS"
1150  IF VAL(MID$(TI$,4,1))>2 THEN 1350
1160  INPUT "DIRECTION (UP,DOWN, RIGHT)";DI$
1170  IF DI$="U" THEN UP=-1 RI=0 GOTO 1210
1180  IF DI$="D" THEN UP=1:RI=0 GOTO 1210
1190  IF DI$="R" THEN UP=0:RI=1 GOTO 1210
1200  GOTO 1120
1210  INPUT "DISTANCE";DI
1220  PRINT LEFT$(UD$,RO)SPC(CO)"O"
1230  FOR C=1 TO DI
1240  RO=RO+UP
1250  CO=CO+RI
1260  FOR AS=1 TO 50
1270  IF CO=AC(AS) AND RO=DO(AS) THEN 1370
1280  IF CO=AC(AS) AND RO=DO(AS)+1 THEN 1370
1285  IF CO=AC(AS)+1 AND RO=DO(AS)+1 THEN 370
1290  NEXT AS
1300  IF RO>24 OR RO<4 THEN 1390
1310  PRINT LEFT$(UD$,RO)SPC(CO)"O"
1320  IF CO>33 THEN 1410
1330  NEXT C
1340  GOTO 1110
1350  PRINT "▓◧◧◧◧◧◧◧◧◧◧◧         YOU HAVE RUN OUT OF
      FUEL"
1360  PRINT "▓▓     AND WILL DRIFT IN SPACE FOR EVER"
      :STOP
1370  PRINT "▓◧◧◧◧◧◧◧◧◧◧◧    YOU HAVE CRASHED INTO AN
      ASTEROID"
1380  PRINT "▓▓   AND YOUR SHIP IS TERMINALLY DAMAGED"
      :STOP
1390  PRINT "▓◧◧◧◧◧◧◧◧◧◧◧        YOU HAVE GONE OUT OF
      ORBIT"
1400  PRINT "▓▓        AND ARE LOST IN SPACE":STOP
1410  PRINT "▓◧◧◧◧◧◧◧◧◧◧◧      WELL DONE! YOU MISSED THEM
      ALL!"
1420  PRINT "▓▓       YOU QUALIFY AS A SHUTTLE PILOT"
1430  F$="LANDING"
1440  GOSUB3000
2000  REM LANDER
2010  PRINT"◧"
2020  D=18000:S=400:H=2000:F=5
2030  C$="       "
2035  UD$="◧◧◧◧◧◧◧◧◧◧◧◧◧◧◧◧◧◧◧◧◧◧◧◧"
2040  PRINT"◪  HEIGHT  ◪DESCENT  ◪SPEED  ◪DISTANCE"
2050  PRINTLEFT$(UD$,24)SPC(35)"▉▉  "
2060  X=0:Y=3
2070  PRINTLEFT$(UD$,Y+1)SPC(X)"▉▉▉"
2080  PRINT"◧◧◧◧    "C$
2090  PRINT"◧◧◧◧◧"H
2100  PRINT"◧◧◧◧"SPC(13)C$
2110  PRINT"◤◧◧◧◧"SPC(13)F
2120  PRINT"◧◧◧◧"SPC(20)C$
2130  PRINT"◧◧◧◧"SPC(20)S
2140  PRINT"◧◧◧◧"SPC(27)C$
2150  PRINT"▉◧◧◧◧"SPC(27)D
2160  IF S<200 THEN PRINT LEFT$(UD$,11)SPC(12)"◪SHUTTLE
      STALLED":STOP
2170  IF D<-999 THEN PRINT LEFT$(UD$,11)"◪ SHUTTLE HAS
      OVERSHOT THE RUNWAY":STOP
2180  IF H<=0 THEN 2290
2190  GET R$
2200  IF R$="A" THEN F=F+1:S=S+5
2210  IF R$="D" THEN F=F-1:S=S-5
2220  IF F=0 THEN F=1:S=S-20
2230  H=H-F:S=S+(F-5)*3:D=D-INT(S/10)
2240  PRINT LEFT$(UD$,Y+1)SPC(X)C$
2250  X=35-INT(D/(18000/35))
2260  Y=22-INT(H/(2000/19))
2270  PRINT LEFT$(UD$,Y+1)SPC(X)"▉▉▉"
2280  GOTO2080
2290  IF D>1000 THEN PRINT LEFT$(UD$,11)"◪       LANDING
      SHORT OF RUNWAY":END
2300  IF S>300 THEN PRINT LEFT$(UD$,11)"◪       LANDING
      SPEED TOO HIGH":END
2310  IF F>5 THEN PRINT LEFT$(UD$,11)
      "◪     UNDERCARRIAGE COLLAPSED":END
2320  PRINT LEFT$(UD$,11)"◪      WELL DONE, A PERFECT
      LANDING!!!":END
3000  REM LINK
3010  FOR D=1 TO 5000
3020  NEXT D
3030  POKE54276,129
3040  PRINT"◧"
3050  FOR L=1 TO 20
3060  PRINT"    ◪◪ALERT!! "F$" FIELD AHEAD!!!◧"
3070  NEXT L
3080  FOR D=1 TO 8000
3090  NEXT D
3095  POKE54276,128
3100  RETURN
```

Glossary

Array An array is a set of data, held together and identified by one variable name (see also the entry for *variable*). One way of imagining an array is as a series of boxes within the computer's memory, with each separate piece of data held in a separate box.

CHR$** All the symbols and numbers on the computer's keyboard have a numerical **CHR$ code. You can find out what they are by asking the computer to "**PRINT CHR$ 87**", for example.

Delay Delays are sometimes included in computer programs when it is necessary to slow the computer down. They are usually part of a **FOR.....NEXT** loop (see below) and look like this in a program:
FOR DE = 1 TO 1000: NEXT DE.
This would cause the computer to count to 1000 before going on to the next stage of the program.

DIM The BASIC statement for opening an array. It is followed by a number in brackets which tells the computer how big the array should be.

FOR.....NEXT This is a sequence of commands that are used to make the computer repeat an operation a certain number of times. For example, the command:
FOR x=1 TO 5:PRINT 2*x:NEXT x
would cause the computer to **PRINT** the two times table up to five.

GET This instruction is used to send the computer to the keyboard to check to see if any key has been pressed. The exact instruction varies between different models of computer.

GOTO This statement tells the computer to go to the specified line, missing out any lines in-between. It is usually used with **IF.....THEN** (see below) and is only operated if certain conditions are true. Be careful when using **GOTO**s, as it's easy to have the program jumping backward and forward so much that it is impossible to read.

IF.....THEN This is used as a way of telling the computer to do something only when certain conditions are true. This instruction often looks something like this: **IF** score=10 **THEN PRINT** "WELL DONE, YOU'VE WON!!!"

INPUT This instruction allows the computer to be given information while a program is running. When the computer comes to an **INPUT** instruction it prints a question mark (or, for some computers, a different symbol) to prompt the user, and waits for the input to be given.

INT **INT** is short for integer, and instructs the computer to make a whole number of a figure with decimal places in it. It is often used in conjunction with the **RND** command which instructs the computer to generate a random number (see below).

LET This is one way of giving the computer information. In some programs there may be statements such as: **X**=**10**
This simply means that the number ten is stored under the label X. It is often clearer to write:
LET X=10
The **LET** statement also gives rise to something that at first sight seems illogical, if not impossible. In many programs you will see things like:
LET X=X+1
Of course, in mathematical terms X can't equal X+1. All this type of statement means is "increase the value of whatever is stored in X by one."

LIST This makes the computer display whatever program it has in its memory. You can **LIST** single lines, or parts of a program by following the **LIST** command with the appropriate line numbers.

PRINT This tells the computer to display something on the screen. Letters and symbols that are to be displayed should be enclosed in quotation marks, but numbers need not be.

RND This instruction makes the computer generate a random number. The precise instruction varies between different models of computer. Both the Apple IIe and the Commodore 64 generate random decimal numbers between 0 and 1. To make whole numbers between a desired range this is multiplied by a suitable figure and made a whole number using **INT**.

STEP The **STEP** statement is always used following a **FOR....** statement. It indicates the amount that the variable should be changed for each operation. For example: **FOR X=0 TO 20 STEP 5: PRINT X: NEXT X** Would mean that **X** would rise in steps of five, so that the computer would print 0,5, 10, 15, 20.

Variables When you give the computer information you have to give it a label under which it is stored. This label is called a variable since the information it contains may change during the course of the program. When you want the computer to do something with the information, you must refer to it by its label – its variable name. For example, the statement **LET A**=6 places 6 under the variable name **A**.

There are two types of variable. A *numeric variable* is one in which the information stored will always be numbers. If the data to be stored consists of letters or words then a *string variable* must be used. The variable name must then be followed by the string sign – **$**. So, for example, if you wanted a name stored, the statement would read: **LET N$**="JAMES". String variable information must always be in quotes.

Index

Design
Cooper · West

Program editors
Steve Rodgers
Marcus Milton

Illustrator
Andy Farmer

PRINTED IN BELGIUM BY
proost
INTERNATIONAL BOOK PRODUCTION